I SMELL A POP QUIZ!

A BIG NATE BOOK
by Lincoln Peirce

United Media
United Feature Syndicate • Newspaper Enterprise Association
New York

I DON'T REALLY GET LABOR DAY. WHAT'S THE POINT?

WHAT'S THE POINT? IT'S A GREAT HOLIDAY!

IT'S A CELEBRATION OF THE WORKERS THAT MAKE THIS COUNTRY GREAT! THE BUILDERS! THE PLUMBERS! THE TRUCK DRIVERS!...

...AAAAAANNNNND!...

DON'T SAY IT. DON'T SAY IT!

...THE SCHOOL TEACHERS!

YAAH!

When school let out,
What did they do?
Can you perhaps recall?

They shook your hand,
They smiled and said:
"We'll see you kids next fall!"

But fall,
Unless my eyes deceive,
Is sixteen days away.

How come we're hearing
"Welcome back"
On such a summer day?

PRINCIPAL NICHOLS, WHAT'S WITH THE HALL-WAY?

WE HAD ALL THE CORRIDORS REPAINTED!

RESEARCH HAS SHOWN THAT COLORS CAN AFFECT MOOD! SO WE...

WHOA, WHOA! "RESEARCH HAS SHOWN"?

WHAT DOES THAT MEAN? A FEW LAB RATS LOOK AT SOME COLOR SWATCHES, AND ALL OF A SUDDEN WE'VE GOT PINK WALLS?

SO MUCH FOR THE SOOTHING PROPERTIES OF "OCEAN CORAL".

IF YOU WANT TO SPEND MONEY, HOW ABOUT BUMPING UP THE FIELD TRIP BUDGET?

8

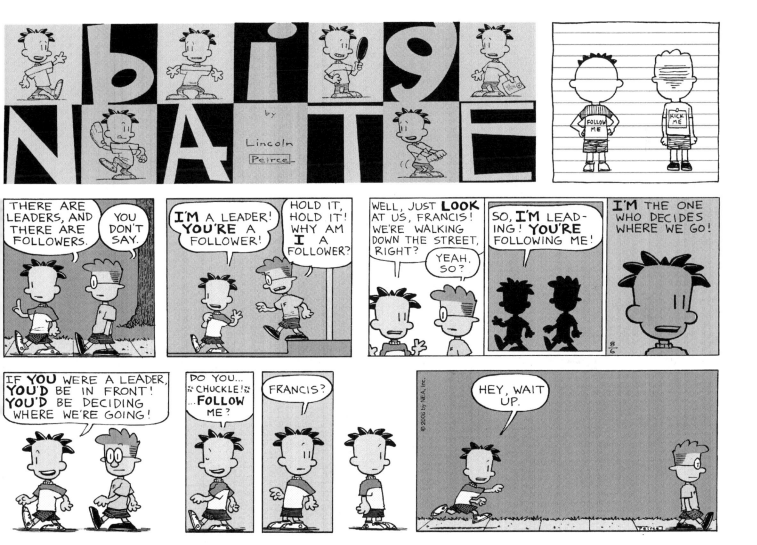

12

13

15

20

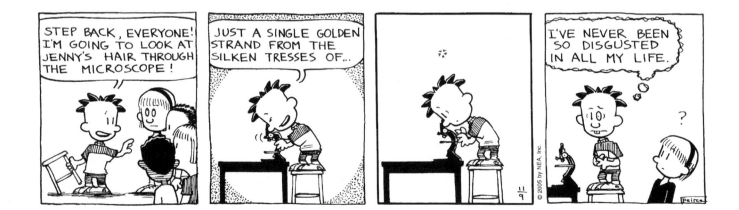

27

31

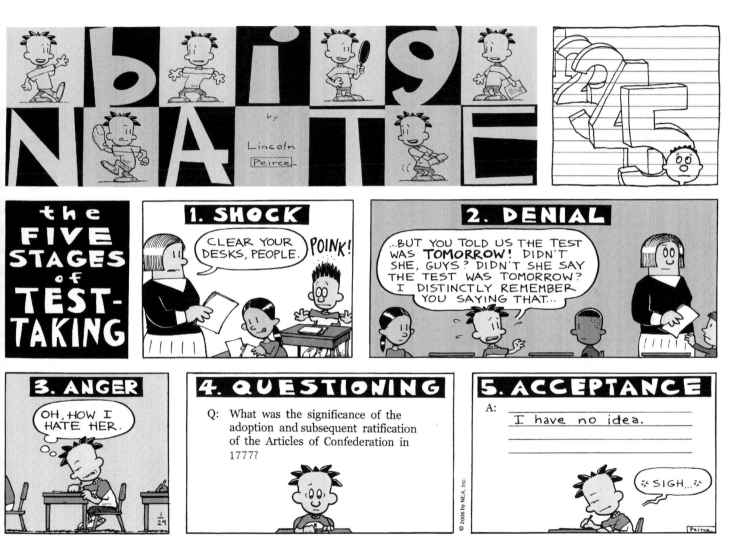

35

39

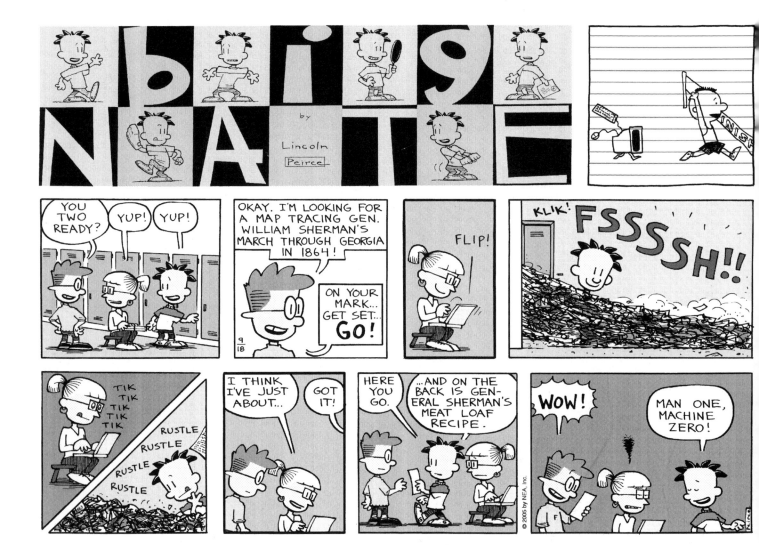

42

44

45

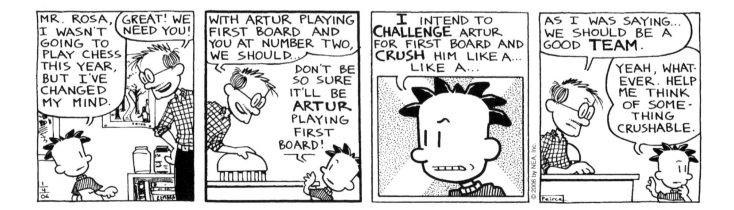

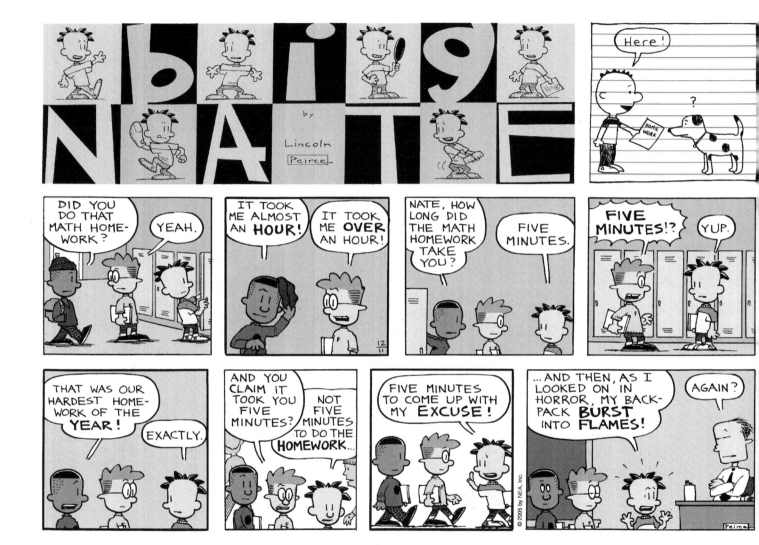

www.comics.com

© 2005 by NEA, Inc.

50

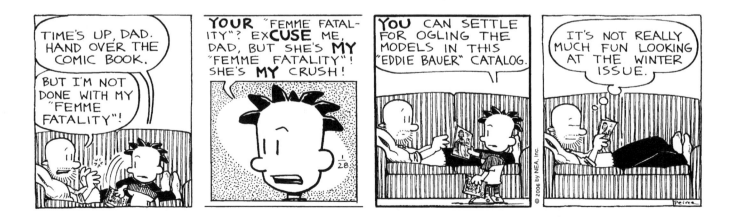

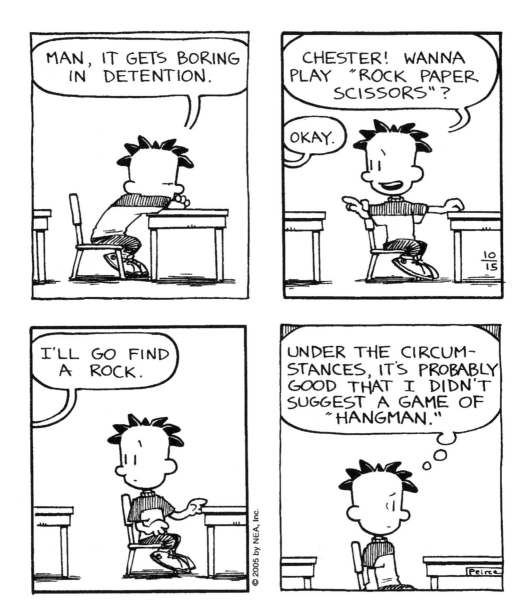

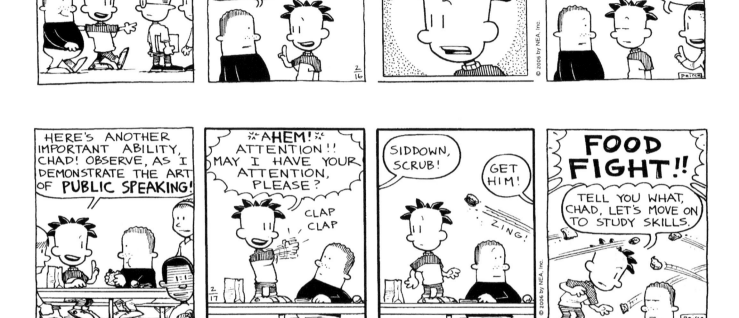

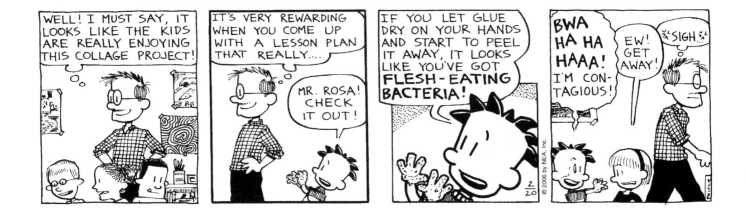

70

NARF NARF CHOMP MUNCH SLOP SLURP MUNCH NARF CHOMPF

MRS. GODFREY EATING ALL DAY IS GROSSING ME OUT.

SHE'S GOT PREGNANCY CRAVINGS! WHAT'S IT TO YOU?

DUDE. YOU'VE GOT FOOD IN YOUR HAIR.

SPEAKING OF PREGNANCY, I THINK I'VE JUST COME DOWN WITH A BAD CASE OF MORNING SICKNESS.

MRS. GODFREY? DO YOU THINK YOU'LL HAVE A BOY OR A GIRL?

I'M NOT SURE!

I'VE BEEN CRAVING SWEET FOODS, WHICH SUPPOSEDLY MEANS I'LL HAVE A **GIRL**...

...BUT LATELY I'VE **ALSO** BEEN CRAVING **SALTY** FOODS, WHICH COULD MEAN I'M HAVING A **BOY**!

OOH! ONE OF EACH!

TWINS!

HIDE MY CHIPS.

I'M PREDICTING YOU'RE GOING TO HAVE A GIRL, MRS. GODFREY!

NOT ME! I'M PREDICTING A BOY!

...AND SINCE YOU ALREADY **HAVE** A GIRL, YOU PROBABLY **WANT** A BOY, RIGHT?

BELCH!

NOT NECESSARILY.

WHOO! PARDON MY NACHOS!

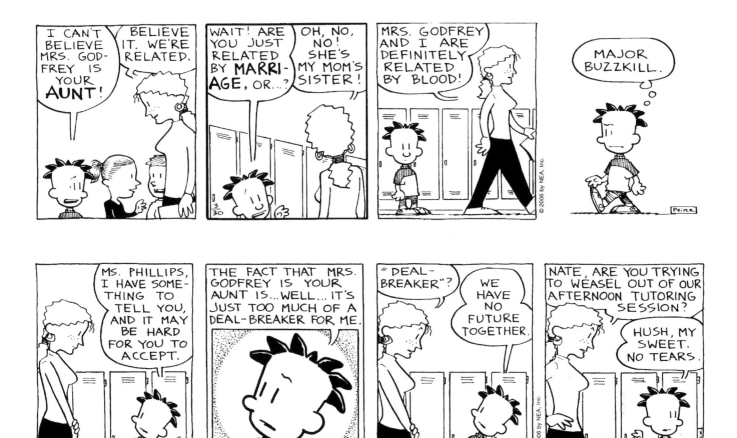

The Boston Tea Party, which took place on December 16, 1773, was a very significant event in United States history.

The Boston Tea Party, which took place on December 16, 1773, was a very significant event in United States history.

To say the colonists were upset with England for taxing their tea is understating the matter. They were BEYOND upset. They were angry, irate, miffed, peeved, mad, furious, perturbed, enraged, ticked off, sore, chafed, cross, huffy, incensed, and generally splenetic.

85

86

96

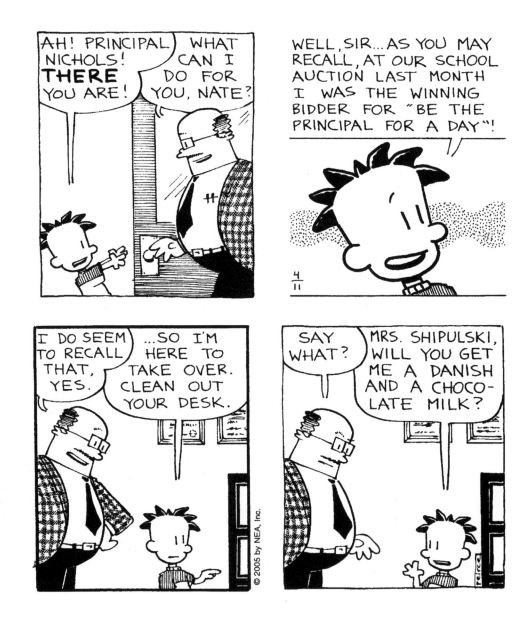

103

105

YES! RIGHT DOWN THE....

7/10

...MIDDLE.

...IF BY "MIDDLE" YOU MEAN THE MEDIAN STRIP OF ROUTE 95.

MULLIGAN.

© 2006 by NEA, Inc.

Peirce

...AND IT'S IN THE CUP! WHAT'D I TAKE ON THIS HOLE?

UH...THAT DEPENDS...

IF YOU COUNT ALL THE LOST BALLS, THE PENALTY STROKES, AND THE TIMES YOU ILLEGALLY IMPROVED YOUR LIE, THEN IT'S A TWENTY-THREE.

IF, ON THE OTHER HAND, YOU COMPLETELY DIS-REGARD THE RULES OF GOLF, THEN IT'S A FIVE.

7/11

© 2006 by NEA, Inc.

LET'S SPLIT THE DIFFERENCE AND CALL IT A SIX!

THAT SEEMS FAIR.

Peirce

HOW COME EVERYBODY CHEATS AT GOLF?

I MEAN, YOU DON'T SEE PEOPLE CHEAT-ING AT BOWLING!

WELL, YOU CAN'T CHEAT AT BOWLING, NOW THAT ALL THE ALLEYS HAVE ELEC-TRONIC SCORING!

7/12

BACK WHEN PEOPLE KEPT SCORE WITH A PENCIL AND PAPER, IT WAS EASY TO CHEAT!

Peirce

© 2006 by NEA, Inc.

GREAT, DAD. NICE ROLE MODELING.

OOP! GET OUT OF THE ROUGH, YOU RASCAL!

KICK!

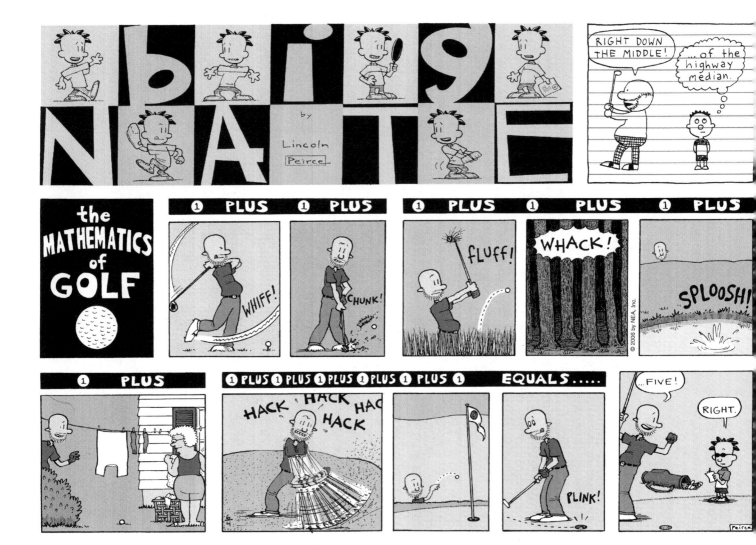

112

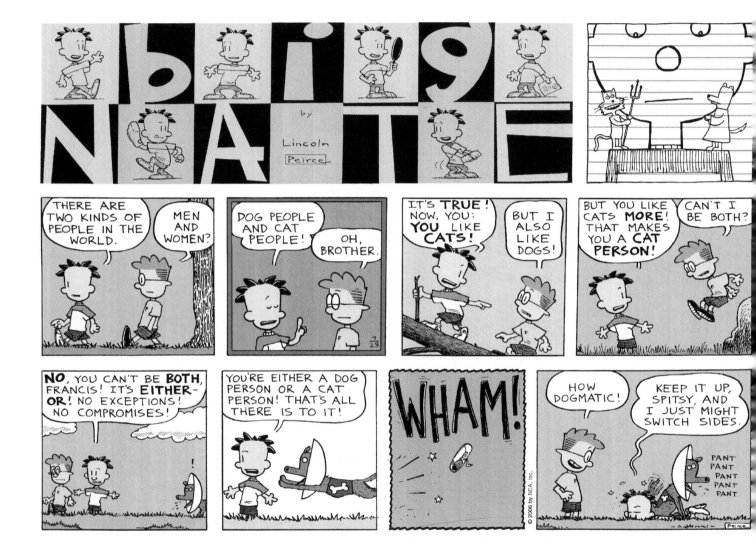

124

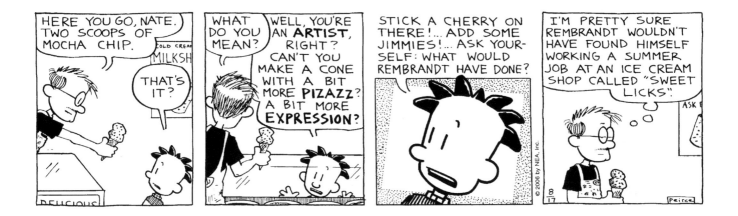

126